NYLON

INVESTIGATE MATERIALS

Contents

HOW TO USE THIS BOOK

Before reading with your child it will be helpful to look through the book together and talk about the cover, pictures, and new challenge words. This story is called nylon. Let's read the book to find out about nylon, where it comes from, and how we use it.

Challenge Words

nylon: man-made plastic thread.

material: something used to make fabric or other items.

fabric: cloth.

man-made: something that is made by people and is not found in nature.

factory: a place where machines make things.

thread: a long, thin piece of cotton, nylon, or other material used to knit or weave fabric.

weave: to push thread over and under rows of thread to make fabric.

knit: to make loops of thread and join the loops to make fabric.

pattern: a shape or design that decorates something.

magnifying glass: a glass you look through that makes things look bigger.

dye: to change the color of something.

silky: shiny, soft, and smooth.

silk: the thread from the cocoons of silkworms.

What is nylon?

Nylon is a **material**. A material is used to make something. We use nylon to make **fabric**.

Where does nylon come from?

Nylon is not found in nature. It is **man-made** from oil found deep under the ground.

How is nylon made into fabric?

5

The oil goes to a **factory** where it is turned into plastic **thread**. Nylon is thread that is plastic.

Nylon thread is ready to **weave** or **knit** into fabric.

Weaving is pushing threads over and under other threads. This makes a **pattern**. Knitting is making loops of thread and joining them in a pattern.

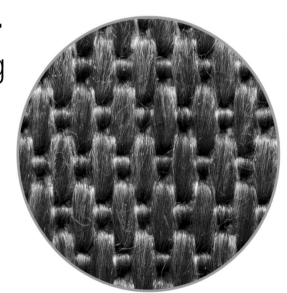

What does nylon look like?

9

Look at nylon through a **magnifying glass**. It is smooth and shiny. Clear nylon can be **dyed** to make different colors.

How does nylon feel?

Nylon feels **silky**, like the bristles of your toothbrush. Nylon is even called man-made **silk**.

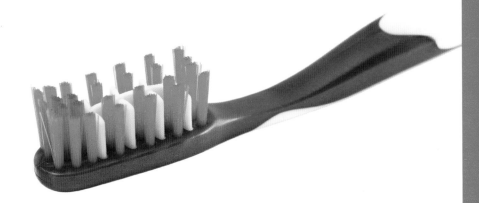

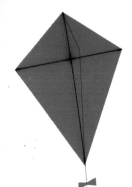

Why do we use nylon?

Nylon is easy to clean and dries fast. It doesn't get wrinkly. When you sleep in a tent, nylon fabric keeps you warm and dry.

Nylon is lightweight and stretchy.
Nylon is so strong it is
even used to make
ropes for big ships.

What do YOU have that is made from nylon?

17

Maybe you keep dry under a nylon umbrella, or swim in a nylon bathing suit. A nylon seatbelt keeps you safe. You fly a nylon kite.

19

Maybe someday you'll take a ride
in a nylon hot air balloon.
Or skydive with a nylon parachute.

Now that you know about nylon,
you will see it everywhere you look!

Nomad Press
A division of Nomad Communications
10 9 8 7 6 5 4 3 2 1

Printed by Regal Printing Limited in China,
June 2011, Job Number 1105034
ISBN: 978-1-936313-97-6

Educational Consultant, Marla Conn

Questions regarding the ordering of this book should be addressed to
Independent Publishers Group
814 N. Franklin St., Chicago, IL 60610
www.ipgbook.com

Nomad Press
2456 Christian St., White River Junction, VT 05001
www.nomadpress.net

Image Credits

©iStockphoto.com/ Elemental Imaging, cover; James Steidl, James Group Studios, title page;
Desuza Communications, 1; Amanda Rohde, Hidesy, 2; Kim Gunkel, 3; Nawaran Sirisunthorn, 4;
Igor Kisselev, 5; AdShooter, 6; Felinda, 7; sgaby, 8; David Hernandez, 9; Antagain, 10; G.M.Vozd, 11;
Windujedi, 12; Sianc Photography, 13; Soren Pilman,14; Peter Booth, Primary Picture, 16;
Mustafa Arican, Foto Graf Deposu, 17; Pathathai Chungyam, Paula Photographic, 18;
Mike Sonnenberg, Huron Photo, 19; Aldegonde Le Compte, 20.

123rf.com/ Guido Vrola, 4.

Corbisimages.com/ Mark Karrass, 16.